Angelology

Understanding Angels

Gregory Brown

B**I**G Publishing

Endorsements

"The Bible Teacher's Guide … will help any teacher study and get a better background for his/her Bible lessons. In addition, it will give direction and scope to teaching of the Word of God. Praise God for this contemporary introduction to the Word of God."

—Dr. Elmer Towns
Co-founder of Liberty University
Former Dean, Liberty Baptist Theological Seminary

"Expositional, theological, and candidly practical! I highly recommend The Bible Teacher's Guide for anyone seeking to better understand or teach God's Word."

—Dr. Young–Gil Kim
Founding President, Handong Global University

"Helpful to both the layman and the serious student, The Bible Teacher's Guide, by Dr. Greg Brown, is outstanding!"

—Dr. Neal Weaver
President, Louisiana Baptist University

"Whether you are preparing a Bible study, a sermon, or simply wanting to dive deeper into a personal study of God's Word, these will be very helpful tools."

—Eddie Byun
Associate Professor of Christian Ministry, Biola University
Author of Justice Awakening

"I am happy that Greg is making his insights into God's truth available to a wider audience through these books. They bear the hallmarks of good Bible teaching: the result of rigorous Bible study and thoroughgoing application to the lives of people."

—Ajith Fernando
Teaching Director, Youth for Christ
Author of A Call to Joy and Pain

"The content of the series is rich. My prayer is that God will use it to help the body of Christ grow strong."

—Dr. Min Chung
Senior Pastor, Covenant Fellowship Church, Urbana, Illinois
Adjunct Professor, Urbana Theological Seminary

"Knowing the right questions to ask and how to go about answering them is fundamental to learning in any subject matter. Greg demonstrates this convincingly."

—Dr. William Moulder
Professor of Biblical Studies, Trinity International University

"Pastor Greg is passionate about the Word of God, rigorous and thorough in his approach to the study of it... I am pleased to recommend The Bible Teacher's Guide to anyone who hungers for the living Word."

—Dr. JunMo Cho
Professor of Linguistics, Handong Global University
Contemporary Christian Music Recording Artist

"I can't imagine any student of Scripture not benefiting by this work."

—Steven J. Cole
Pastor, Flagstaff Christian Fellowship, Flagstaff, Arizona
Author of the Riches from the Word series

"Greg deals with the principles, doctrines, and applications of the text in a practical way which is useful for both individual growth or for help in preparation for teaching."

—Bob Deffinbaugh
Ministry Coordinator, Bible.org
Founding Pastor, Community Bible Chapel, Richardson, Texas

Content

Preface

And entrust what you heard me say in the presence of many others as witnesses to faithful people who will be competent to teach others as well.
2 Timothy 2:2 (NET)

Paul's words to Timothy still apply to us today. The church needs teachers who clearly and fearlessly teach the Word of God. With this in mind, The Bible Teacher's Guide (BTG) series was created. This series includes both expositional and topical studies, with resources to help teachers lead small groups, pastors prepare sermons, and individuals increase their knowledge of God's Word.

Angelology can be used for personal study or as a four to six-session small group curriculum, depending on how the leader divides up the topics. For small groups, the members will read a chapter (or chapters) and discuss the reflection questions and anything else that stood out in the reading within their gathering. Or, the chapter can be read before the gathering, with the meeting focusing only on discussion.

Introduction

What are angels? Who are they and what can we learn from them? In Scripture, angels are mentioned over 250 times[1] in thirty-four books of the Bible (seventeen in the Old Testament and seventeen in the New Testament).[2] Angels were present, rejoicing at God's forming of the earth (Job 38:4-7). They visited Abraham's house and brought judgment on Sodom and Gomorrah (Gen 18, 19:13). They were involved with the transmission of the Ten Commandments to Moses (Gal 3:19). An angel gave prophecies to Daniel about Israel's future (Dan 9, 10). Likewise, an angel prophesied the messiah's birth to both Mary and Joseph (Matt 1, Lk 1). An angel strengthened Christ after he experienced temptation in the wilderness (Lk 22:43). An angel set Peter free from prison (Acts 12:7-10), and one comforted Paul before his shipwreck in the ocean (Acts 27:23-24). Angels will be involved with administering judgment throughout the Great Tribulation (Rev 8) and will come with Christ to judge the earth (Matt 16:27). Throughout Scripture, angels are everywhere.

The study of angels is not just speculative; we can learn a great deal from them, as they are fellow servants and worshipers of God (Rev 22:9). Here are several reasons to study angels.

1. The existence of angels and their ministry give us an example to follow.

In the Lord's Prayer, Christ taught us to pray, "may your kingdom come, may your will be done on earth as it is in heaven"

(Matt 6:10). In that sense, angels are an example to us. They are examples to follow in the way they worship and serve God in heaven. May their example be followed here on earth!

2. The existence of angels and their ministry should give great comfort to believers.

In 2 Kings 6:17, when Elisha and his servant were surrounded by a pagan army, God opened the eyes of the servant to see an army of angels protecting them. Likewise, angels protect us. In Psalm 91:10-12, the Psalmist said: "No harm will overtake you; no illness will come near your home. For he will order his angels to protect you in all you do. They will lift you up in their hands, so you will not slip and fall on a stone." Likewise, in Matthew 18:10, Christ said, "See that you do not disdain one of these little ones. For I tell you that their angels in heaven always see the face of my Father in heaven." God is always protecting his saints through the agency of angels, which should give believers great comfort.

3. The existence of angels should sober us in our fight against sin.

The angels were made perfect and holy and were never tempted by an outside force as the first humans were, and yet some fell into sin. As we'll see, one-third of the angels rebelled against God (Rev 12:4). If perfect angels can sin against God without a sin nature and outside forces tempting them, how much more vulnerable are we who have a sin nature, the world, and demons to tempt us (Jam 1:14, John 2:16, Eph 6:12-13)? First Corinthians 10:12 says, "So let the one who thinks he is standing be careful that he does not fall." Angels encourage us to be sober in our fight against sin.

4. The existence of angels and their ministry should humble us and make us thankful that God chose to offer us salvation, even though he did not have to.

When one-third of the angels fell, forgiveness was never offered to them. In God's fore-planning, he chose for Christ to die for humans, but not angels. This reality should humble us and make us grateful for the amazing grace God has shown to humans. Ephesians 2:8-9 says, "For by grace you are saved through faith, and this is not from yourselves, it is the gift of God; it is not from works, so that no one can boast."

5. The existence of angels and their ministry reminds us that there is a real unseen world that greatly affects the seen world.

There is an unseen battle happening in the heavenlies between angels and demons, which affects the world (Dan 10:12-13, 20-21). In fact, believers, as fellow servants of God, engage in this battle with Satan and demons. In Ephesians 6:12-13, Paul said, "For our struggle is not against flesh and blood, but against the rulers, against the powers, against the world rulers of this darkness, against the spiritual forces of evil in the heavens."

In Angelology, we will consider many questions about angels, including who they are, their creation, types of angels, specific angels, their ministry, their future, and much more.

Reflection

1. What stood out most in the reading and why?
2. What are some examples of angels appearing in Scripture?
3. What are some reasons to study angels?

4. What other questions or applications did you take from the reading?

Angelic Titles

What are titles or names for angels in Scripture? By considering their titles, we learn something about their character and purpose.

Messengers

In both the Old and New Testament, the words used for angels (malak and angelos) simply mean messenger[3] —one who is sent to act and speak for another.[4] In Scripture, they are commonly seen giving messages to people from God and acting on behalf of him. In Daniel 9, Daniel receives a prophetic message from an angel about the future of Israel (v. 20-27). And, the entire book of Revelation is given to John by an angel. Revelation 1:1 says, "The revelation of Jesus Christ, which God gave him to show his servants what must happen very soon. He made it clear by sending his angel to his servant John." Angels are messengers from God.

Sons of God

In the Old Testament, angels are commonly called "sons of God" (Job 1:6, 2:1, 38:7). Job 1:6 says, "Now the day came when the sons of God came to present themselves before the LORD—and Satan also arrived among them." The title "sons of God" pictures how God is the father of angels. The same title is used of Adam in Matthew's genealogy of Christ because Adam was created by God in his likeness (Matt 3:38; cf. Gen 1:26-28). Though angels are never said to be made in God's image as humans are, they may in fact be made in God's image, as the title "sons of God" suggests (cf. Gen 5:3). Certainly, in some ways, they bear God's characteristics more than humans. They are stronger, wiser, more powerful, and have greater authority than humans. For a season, humans were made a little "lower than the angels" (Heb 2:7). With that said, apparently after Christ's coming, believers will judge angels and therefore be in authority over them (1 Cor 6:3; cf. Eph 1:20-22, 2:6). It seems that in the same way God placed humans on the earth to rule (Gen 1:28), angels were placed in the heavenlies to rule. Consider these verses that describe their ruling function: Ephesians 3:10 says, "The purpose of this enlightenment is that through the church the multifaceted wisdom of God should now be disclosed to the rulers and the authorities in the heavenly realms." Also, Colossians 1:16 says,

> for all things in heaven and on earth were created by him—all things, whether visible or invisible, whether thrones or dominions, whether principalities or powers—all things were created through him and for him.

Angels are sons of God; they are called to rule the heavens under God, even as humans are called to rule the earth under God.

Holy Ones

In Scripture, angels are at times called "holy ones." In Psalm 89:5 and 7 (ESV), the Psalmist says,

> Let the heavens praise your wonders, O LORD, your faithfulness in the assembly of the holy ones! ... a God greatly to be feared in the council of the holy ones, and awesome above all who are around him?

Angels are holy because they were created to be pure and righteous, and because they attend to the holiness of God. In Isaiah

6:3, the angels in the presence of God continually cry out, "Holy, Holy, Holy is the Lord who commands armies!"

Hosts

Angels are at times called "hosts" (Ps 89:6, Is 31:4, 1 Sam 17:45), which refers to them as God's heavenly army. First Samuel 17:45 says,

> But David replied to the Philistine, "You are coming against me with sword and spear and javelin. But I am coming against you in the name of the LORD of hosts, the God of Israel's armies, whom you have defied!

Angels often fight God's battles on behalf of believers against demons and evil people (Dan 10:20-21, 12:1, Heb 1:14).

Watchers

Angels are at times called "watchers" (Dan 4:13, 17, 23). Daniel 4:13 (ESV) says, "I saw in the visions of my head as I lay in bed, and behold, a watcher, a holy one, came down from heaven." This term pictures them as watching God's activity throughout the earth and specifically watching humans. Further evidence of their watching activity is demonstrated in the following verses: In 1 Corinthians 4:9, Paul said, "For, I think, God has exhibited us apostles last of all, as men condemned to die, because we have become a spectacle to the world, both to angels and to people." Likewise, Peter spoke specifically about how angels watch believers to learn about the implications of the gospel. First Peter 1:12 says,

> They were shown that they were serving not themselves but you, in regard to the things now announced to you through those who proclaimed the gospel to you by the

Holy Spirit sent from heaven—things angels long to catch a glimpse of.

Why do angels watch humans so intently? As mentioned, it seems they are particularly interested in understanding the practical applications of salvation. Some have speculated that since the angels were never offered grace and mercy after some rebelled against God, they have a strong understanding of God's holiness, wrath, and justice, but little understanding of God's grace and mercy—God's underserved and unmerited favor. They, no doubt, understand these mentally but not experientially. They learn about the out-workings of salvation from humans, and since knowing and honoring God is their chief function, they are intensely interested in understanding it. Charles Ryrie's comments on this are helpful:

> Probably the statements about angels observing the conduct of redeemed people startle our thinking as much as any of these truths. The reason for their interest in us may stem from the fact that since angels do not personally experience salvation, the only way they can see the effects of salvation is to observe how it is manifest in saved human beings. We are indeed a theater in which the world, men, and angels make up the audience (1 Cor. 4:9). Let us put on a good performance for them as well as for the Lord before whom all things are naked and open.[5]

In Ephesians 2:7 and 3:10, Paul sheds more light on this reality, as he describes how God uses the church to teach angels:

> to demonstrate in the coming ages the surpassing wealth of his grace in kindness toward us in Christ Jesus ... The purpose of this enlightenment is that through the church the multifaceted wisdom of God should now be disclosed to the rulers and the authorities in the heavenly realms.

Angels are watchers because they study God's work in redeemed humans to learn more about God and worship him more thoroughly.

Conclusion

Angels are messengers as they speak God's Word and act on behalf of him. They are sons of God because they were created by him and reflect his likeness in various ways. They rule the heavens even as humans rule the earth. They are holy ones because they have been set apart by God to be righteous and attend to his holiness. They are hosts because they fight God's battles. And finally, they are watchers as they study redeemed humanity to understand God's grace—his unmerited favor on behalf of those who are undeserving.

Reflection

1. What stood out most in the reading and why?
2. What are some angelic titles in Scripture and what do they mean or represent?
3. Are angels made in the image of God? Why or why not?
4. Why do angels watch believers?
5. What other questions or applications did you take from the reading?

Characteristics of Angels

What are characteristics of angels? We've considered some by considering the titles used of angels; however, Scripture teaches much more about them.

Angels Are Created Beings

It is clear that angels, like humans, were created by God. Psalm 148:2 and 5 says: "Praise him, all his angels! Praise him, all his heavenly assembly! ... Let them praise the name of the LORD, for he gave the command and they came into existence." With that said, Scripture does not explicitly say when they were created; however, it appears they were created early in the original six days of creation. Exodus 20:11 says: "For in six days the LORD made the heavens and the earth and the sea and all that is in them, and he rested on the seventh day." Everything within the heavens, including angels, were created within the first six days. Also, Genesis 2:1 (ESV) implies the same thing: "Thus the heavens and the earth were finished, and all the *host* of them." Host is a word commonly used of angels.

In addition, Job 38:4-7 indicates that angels were present at the forming of the earth, early on day one of creation. In it, God says to Job:

Where were you when I laid the foundation of the earth? Tell me, if you possess understanding! Who set its measurements—if you know— or who stretched a measuring line across it? On what were its bases set, or who laid its cornerstone—when the morning stars sang in chorus, and all the sons of God shouted for joy?

This may be further implied by Genesis 1:1-2, as Wayne Grudem describes:

There may be a hint at the creation of angelic beings on the first day of creation when we read that "in the beginning God created the heavens and the earth" (Gen. 1:1), and then immediately after we read that "the earth was without form and void" (Gen. 1:2), but with no mention of the heavens in this second verse. This may suggest that the uninhabitable state of the earth is contrasted with the heavens where, perhaps, God had already created angelic beings and assigned them various roles and orders. This idea is made more plausible when we read that "the morning stars sang together, and all the sons of God shouted for joy" at the time when God laid the "cornerstone" of the earth and sunk its "bases" in the process of forming or founding it (Job 38:6–7). If the angels ("the sons of God") shouted for joy when God was making the earth inhabitable, this could imply that God created the angelic beings early on the first day.[6]

Number of Angels

How many angels did God create? Again, Scripture does not clearly say. In Matthew 22:30, Christ said this about humans and their resurrection, "For in the resurrection they neither marry nor are given in marriage, but are like angels in heaven." Therefore, since angels weren't made to marry and procreate, the implication is that their number is fixed. In addition, since they are immortal, no angels will die. Luke 20:36, again comparing resurrected humans to angels, said, "In fact, they can no longer die, because they are equal to angels and are sons of God, since they are sons of the resurrection."

With that said, the actual number of angels seems to be vast and innumerable. Revelation 5:11, in describing the heavenly worship of angels and twenty-four human elders, says:

> Then I looked and heard the voice of many angels in a circle around the throne, as well as the living creatures and the elders. Their number was *ten thousand times ten thousand—thousands times thousands*

There were ten thousand times ten thousand angels. In Hebrews 12:22, the angels worshiping God are said to be "innumerable" (ESV).

Some have speculated that the number of angels is equal to the stars, since angels are at times called stars. Job 38:7 says, "when the morning stars sang in chorus, and all the sons of God shouted for joy?" Also, Revelation 12:4 says, "Now the dragon's tail swept away a third of the stars in heaven and hurled them to the earth." If that is true, that means there are trillions of angels who worship God and serve people.

In considering demonic angels, which isn't the focus of this study, it is notable that one man potentially had 6,000 demons assigned to him. When Christ demanded to know the name of the demoniac in Mark 5:9, the demons responded, "My name is Legion, for we are many." A legion typically consisted of 6,000 men.[7] If Satan can spare 6,000 demons for one human, their number must be vast. Therefore, the total number of angels must be too many to count.

The Fall of Angels

Sometime after angels were created, they experienced a fall, as Satan, one of the chief angels, led one-third of the angels in rebellion against God (Ez 28:14 ESV, Rev 12:3-4, Lk 10:18).

Apparently, like humans, angels had a probation period where they were supposed to demonstrate their obedience to God (cf. Gen 2:16-17). During that period, angels were holy but still able to sin. However, after the fall, fallen angels (demons) are now not able to not sin, even as fallen humans. The angels that did not rebel are called "elect" and are now not able to sin (1 Tim 5:21).

As mentioned, the angelic rebellion was led by Satan, who originally was a high-ranking angel who became prideful and desired to be like God (Is 14:12-15, Ez 28:11-19, 1 Tim 3:6). Satan and demons will be more thoroughly considered in Satanology instead of Angelology.

Angels Are Spirit Beings

Unlike humans who have a material body, angels are immaterial beings. In Scripture, they are called "spirits." Hebrews 1:14 says this about holy angels, "Are they not all ministering spirits, sent out to serve those who will inherit salvation?" Evil angels are at times called evil or unclean spirits (Luke 8:2; 11:24, 26). Luke 8:2 says, "and also some women who had been healed of *evil spirits* and disabilities: Mary (called Magdalene), from whom seven demons had gone out." And, in Ephesians 2:2, Satan is called "the spirit that is now at work in the sons of disobedience."

Though angels are spirits, in Scripture, they at times appear as humans when accomplishing a mission. Every time this happens, they take on male form. Three men visited Abraham's home in Genesis 18—two of them were angels and one was God. In Daniel 10:5, a male angel appeared to Daniel to share with him about the future of Israel, including the kingdoms that would rule over her. With that said, there is one time in Scripture where angels might appear as females; however, it is inconclusive. In a vision in Zechariah 5:9-11, two women with wings take a basket filled with wickedness to Babylon. Verse 9 says, "Then I looked again and saw two women going forth with the wind in their wings (they had wings like those of a stork) and they lifted up the basket between the earth and the sky."

It should be noted that though angels are spirit beings like God (John 4:24)—meaning they have no material nature—they are finite beings and not infinite beings like God. As creatures, they are limited. They are not omnipresent—they cannot be in more than one place at once. They are not omniscient—they do not know all things, including what we are thinking. And they are not omnipotent—though powerful, they are not all-powerful. They are finite.

Angels Are Personal Beings

Angels are personal beings in that they demonstrate the qualities of personhood—intellect, emotion, and will. Their intellect is demonstrated in their ability to carry out God's commands and converse with humans. No doubt, they have greater intellects than humans. (1) Certainly, this is true because they were created in a higher position than humans, and therefore they innately know more. As mentioned, Hebrews 2:7 says, humans were made "lower than the angels for a little while." (2) Also, angels have existed since the original creation, allowing them to observe and learn more than humans.

Furthermore, angels demonstrate emotions. In Luke 15:10, Jesus described how the angels rejoice when a sinner repents. He said, "In the same way, I tell you, there is joy in the presence of God's angels over one sinner who repents." Finally, angels demonstrate will in that the holy angels chose to obey God and not follow Satan, while the demons chose to rebel against God. With that said, like all creatures, angels are subject to God's will. Ephesians 1:11 says God "accomplishes all things according to the counsel of his will." Angels submit to and obey God's will as their first priority. Demons must submit to God's sovereign will as well, which is a mystery. Even Satan had to get permission from God to tempt and try Job (Job 1:12, 2:6), and at times, we see demons explicitly obey God in Scripture. In 1 Samuel 16:14, God sends an evil spirit to torment Saul because of his disobedience, and in 1 Kings 22:22, a lying spirit is sent by God to deceive King Ahab, so God could destroy him (v. 20). These are mysteries which demonstrate God's sovereignty over all his creation (Eph 1:11, Col 1:17).

Angels Are Glorious Beings

Since angels are "sons of God" and display aspects of his image, this is seen in how glorious they are. When angels appear in Scripture, they are often magnificent in appearance and revealed in a shining light. Consider Daniel 10:5-6, which details Daniel seeing an angel. It says,

> I looked up and saw a man clothed in linen; around his waist was a belt made of gold from Upaz. His body resembled yellow jasper, and his face had an appearance like lightning. His eyes were like blazing torches; his arms and feet had the gleam of polished bronze. His voice thundered forth like the sound of a large crowd.

Daniel said the angel's face appeared like "lightning" and his eyes like "blazing torches." The vision was so powerful, Daniel fell to his face and his energy was drained (v. 8-9). Also, in Acts 12:7, when an angel appeared to Peter while he was in prison, it says, "Suddenly an angel of the Lord appeared, and a light shone in the prison cell..." In Luke 2:9, when an angel appeared to the shepherds to announce the birth of Jesus, the text says, "An angel of the Lord appeared to them, and the glory of the Lord shone around them, and they were absolutely terrified." Throughout Scripture, angels are shown to be glorious beings—appearing with great light.

Angels Are Powerful Beings

In Scripture, angels are also seen to be powerful beings, much more powerful than humans. In 2 Peter 2:10-11, Peter talks about how false prophets often boastfully insult fallen angels, though holy angels who are much more powerful do not even do so. He says: "Brazen and insolent, they are not afraid to insult the glorious ones, yet even angels, who are much more powerful, do not bring a slanderous judgment against them before the Lord."

In 2 Samuel 24:15-17, angelic power is seen in how God used a single angel to destroy 70,000 Jewish men as a judgment for David pridefully conducting a census of Israel. Also, in Revelation 7:1, four angels hold "back the four winds of the earth so no wind could blow on the earth, on the sea, or on any tree." Angels have tremendous power, much more than humans.

Angels Are Functional Beings

Angels are functional beings in that they serve God in a variety of ways:

1. Angels worship God.

In Scripture, they are often seen continually praising God for his characteristics and works. Revelation 4:8 describes angels worshiping God day and night. It says,

> Each one of the four living creatures had six wings and was full of eyes all around and inside. They never rest day or night, saying: "Holy Holy Holy is the Lord God, the All-Powerful, Who was and who is, and who is still to come!"

Also, Isaiah says this about two angels in his vision: "They called out to one another, 'Holy, holy, holy is the Lord who commands armies! His majestic splendor fills the entire earth!'" (Is 6:3).

2. Angels execute God's commands.

This includes many things. (1) Angels commonly bring God's judgment. In Acts 12:23, when Herod failed to give praise to God when the Israelites were calling him a god, an angel struck and killed him. In Revelation, angels are seen bringing various judgments on the earth. Revelation 16:1 says, "Then I heard a loud voice from the temple declaring to the seven angels: 'Go and pour out on the earth the seven bowls containing God's wrath.'" (2) Angels at times control (or manifest) the weather in obedience to God (cf. Ez 1:4, 13). Revelation 7:1 says, "After this I saw four angels standing at the four corners of the earth, holding back the four winds of the earth so no wind could blow on the earth, on the sea, or on any tree." Likewise, Hebrews 1:7 (ESV) says, "Of the angels he says, 'He makes his angels winds, and his ministers a flame of fire.'" (3) Angels seem to have a role in guarding and possibly guiding nations (cf. Dan 10:20-21). In Daniel 12:1, Michael, the archangel, is called "the great prince who watches over your people"—referring to Israel. Likewise, two demonic angels are called the "prince of Persia" and the "prince of Greece" in Daniel 10:20. (4) Angels fight against demonic forces (cf. Dan 10:20-21). In Revelation 12:7-8, Michael, the archangel, leads an angelic war against Satan and his demons. Satan and his demons were defeated, removed from heaven, and no longer had access to it. It says:

> Then war broke out in heaven: Michael and his angels fought against the dragon, and the dragon and his angels fought back. But the dragon was not strong enough to prevail, so there was no longer any place left in heaven for him and his angels.

3. Angels minister to believers.

Certainly, this is done in obedience to God as well. Hebrews 1:14 says, "Are they not all ministering spirits, sent out to serve those who will inherit salvation?" (1) They minister to believers by giving God's messages to them and may be involved in enlightening believers when they study Scripture. Galatians 3:19 says they were involved in giving the law to Moses:

Why then was the law given? It was added because of transgressions, until the arrival of the descendant to whom the promise had been made. It was administered through angels by an intermediary.

An angel gave Daniel understanding of future events concerning Israel (Daniel 9 and 10). (2) They at times aid in leading people to Christ. In Acts 8:26, an angel told Philip to go down the road towards Gaza where he eventually met an Ethiopian eunuch and led him to Christ. Likewise, in Acts 10, an angel told a Roman centurion named Cornelius to call for Peter, who shared the gospel with him and his family. (3) They protect believers. In Matthew 18:10, Jesus said, "See that you do not disdain one of these little ones. For I tell you that their angels in heaven always see the face of my Father in heaven." It is not clear whether this refers to each believer having a guardian angel or angels in general that are always ready to respond to God by defending believers. (4) Angels at times strengthen and comfort believers. In Acts 27:23-25, an angel appeared to Paul, telling him that he must arrive in Rome to testify to Caesar, and therefore, God would protect him and the crew of the ship who were lost at sea. Also, in Luke 22:43, when Christ was weary as he prayed in Gethsemane before his death, an angel appeared and strengthened him. It says, "Then an angel from heaven appeared to him and strengthened him." (5) Angels assist in answering the prayers of believers. When Daniel was fasting and praying to understand Israel's future, an angel appeared to answer his prayer. In Daniel 10:12, the angel said, "Don't be afraid, Daniel, for from the very first day you applied your mind to understand and to humble yourself before your God, your words were heard. I have come in response to your words." Also, in Revelation 8:3-5, angels are seen offering the prayers of the saints to God and possibly executing them:

> Another angel holding a golden censer came and was stationed at the altar. A large amount of incense was given to him to offer up, with the prayers of all the saints, on the golden altar that is before the throne. The smoke coming from the incense, along with the prayers of the saints, ascended before God from the angel's hand. Then the angel took the censer, filled it with fire from the altar, and threw it on the earth, and there were crashes of thunder, roaring, flashes of lightning, and an earthquake.

(6) Angels have a role in bringing the spirits of deceased believers into heaven. In Luke 16:22, Christ describes a poor man named Lazarus who died and was taken to Abraham's side by angels. He said, "Now the poor man died and was carried by the angels to Abraham's side."

Angels Are Organized Beings

Angels, both holy and evil ones, are clearly organized. Several verses describe this: Colossians 1:16 describes how Christ created the order in the invisible realm of angels. It says,

> for all things in heaven and on earth were created by him— all things, whether visible or invisible, whether thrones or dominions, whether principalities or powers—all things were created through him and for him.

When Paul says, "whether thrones or dominions, whether principalities or powers," these describe some type of governmental structure amongst angels. Likewise, in Ephesians

6:12, Paul says the same about demonic angels, which no doubt, mimic God's created order. He says, "For our struggle is not against flesh and blood, but against the rulers, against the powers, against the world rulers of this darkness, against the spiritual forces of evil in the heavens." "Rulers," "powers," "world rulers of this darkness," and "spiritual forces of evil," probably represent something like colonels, generals, and presidents. In fact, in Daniel 10:20, as previously mentioned, an angel refers to battling with the "prince of Persia" and the "prince of Greece," who were high-ranking demonic angels. In Daniel 10:13, he refers to a holy angel called Michael who was a "leading prince." He is also called the "archangel" or "chief angel" in Jude 1:9. In Daniel 10, these high-ranking angels were battling in the heavenlies. Consider the verses below:

> However, the prince of the kingdom of Persia was opposing me for twenty-one days. But Michael, one of the leading princes, came to help me, because I was left there with the kings of Persia.
> Daniel 10:13

> He said, "Do you know why I have come to you? Now I am about to return to engage in battle with the prince of Persia. When I go, the prince of Greece is coming.
> Daniel 10:20

Holy angels, no doubt, have organization so they can effectively accomplish God's plans. In considering this, Charles Ryrie gives practical insight for Christians:

> An important practical point emerges from this. Angels are organized; demons are organized; yet Christians, individually and in groups, often feel that it is unnecessary that they be organized. This is especially true when it comes to fighting evil. Believers sometimes feel that they can "go it alone" or expect victory without any prior,

organized preparation and discipline. It is also true when it comes to promoting good. Believers sometimes miss the best because they do not plan and organize their good works.[8]

Conclusion

Scripture teaches us many characteristics about angels: They are created beings, probably created early on the first day of creation, as they rejoiced at the creation of the earth. They are spirit beings, as they don't have material bodies. They are personal beings who demonstrate intellect, will, and emotions. They are glorious beings who often appear in a shining light. They are powerful beings—much more powerful than humans. They are functional beings who worship God, execute his commands, and serve believers. And, finally, they are organized beings, which allows them to effectively serve God and help people.

Reflection

1. What stood out most in the reading and why?
2. What are some of the characteristics of angels?
3. When were angels created and how many are there?
4. What were the circumstances of the angelic fall?
5. What is the difference between a holy angel and an evil angel?
6. What are some of the functions or jobs of holy angels?
7. What other questions or applications did you take from the reading?

Types of Angels

What are the various types of angels in Scripture? Scripture mentions three types: cherubim, seraphim, and living creatures. We will consider each.

Cherubim

Cherubim are mentioned ninety-two times in thirteen different Bible books (Gen, Ex, Num, 1 and 2 Sam, 1 and 2 Kgs, 1 and 2 Chr, Ps, Is, Ez, and Heb).[9] God originally put a cherub outside of the Garden of Eden to keep humans from eating from the tree of life (Gen 3:24). In the ark of the covenant, golden cherubim were placed above the mercy seat—probably symbolic of real cherubim guarding the presence of God. Exodus 25:22 describes this:

> I will meet with you there, and from above the atonement lid, from between the two cherubim that are over the ark of the testimony, I will speak with you about all that I will command you for the Israelites.

In addition, cherubim were part of the curtain decorations in the tabernacle and temple. Exodus 26:1 says, "The tabernacle itself you are to make with ten curtains of fine twisted linen and blue and purple and scarlet; you are to make them with cherubim that are the work of an artistic designer."

In Ezekiel 1, cherubim were present attending to the glory of God but were called "living beings" (v. 19); in Ezekiel 10:15, these same angels were called "cherubim." However, they differ in appearance from the "living beings" or "living creatures" mentioned in Revelation 4. The cherubim have four faces—that of a man, a lion, an ox, and an eagle—four feet like a calf, and four wings. In contrast, living creatures have one face and six wings (Rev 4:7-8). Ezekiel 1:10-11 describes the cherubim:

> Their faces had this appearance: Each of the four had the face of a man, with the face of a lion on the right, the face of an ox on the left and also the face of an eagle. Their wings were spread out above them; each had two wings touching the wings of one of the other beings on either side and two wings covering their bodies.

In Ezekiel 10:14, one of the four faces is said to be that of a "cherub" instead of an ox. Most likely, a cherub's face must look like that of an ox (Ez 1:10, 10:14). Many scholars believe Satan originally was a cherub who guarded the glory of God until he became prideful and rebelled against God. Ezekiel 28:14 (ESV) says, "You were an anointed guardian cherub. I placed you; you were on the holy mountain of God; in the midst of the stones of fire you walked."

The cherubim remind us to be zealous for God's glory, especially in worship. When the Jews were dishonoring God and cheating people, Jesus went into the temple, scattered the coins of money changers, flipped tables, and yelled, "Take these things away from here! Do not make my Father's house a marketplace!" (John 2:16). Likewise, we must be zealous about guarding God's glory in worship—making sure it aligns with God's Word, as God can only be worshiped in spirit and truth (John 4:23). In addition, since Satan originally was a guardian cherub who became prideful and desired to be like God (Is 14:14, 1 Tim 3:6), we must also be warned against ministering for God and yet seeking glory for ourselves. That was the sin of the Pharisees who did their fasting, praying, and giving, all to be seen by people instead of God (Matt

6:1-18). In Matthew 6:1, Christ warned, "Be careful not to display your righteousness merely to be seen by people. Otherwise you have no reward with your Father in heaven." James 4:6 says, "God opposes the proud, but he gives grace to the humble." It is possible to rebel like Satan and thus be judged by God (1 Tim 3:6). Hebrews 10:29-31 says,

> How much greater punishment do you think that person deserves who has contempt for the Son of God, and profanes the blood of the covenant that made him holy, and insults the Spirit of grace? For we know the one who said, "Vengeance is mine, I will repay," and again, "The Lord will judge his people." It is a terrifying thing to fall into the hands of the living God.

Seraphim

Another group of angels only mentioned in Isaiah 6 is the seraphim. The name means "burning ones."[10] The seraphim have six wings: two to fly with, two to cover their feet, and two to cover their faces (Is 6:2). The four wings that cover their face and feet probably demonstrate their great honor and reverence for God's holiness and glory (Ex 3:5). The two wings to fly with are used to serve God.

As demonstrated by Isaiah 6, the seraphim serve two roles: (1) They are consumed with praising the person of God as they continually cry out to one another, "Holy, holy, holy is the Lord who commands armies! His majestic splendor fills the entire earth!" (v. 3). (2) Also, the seraphim cleanse God's people from sin. In Isaiah 6:6-7, they touch Isaiah's mouth with burning coals to cleanse him from sin, so he can be prepared to serve and speak for God (v. 6-9). Obviously, only Christ can cleanse people of sin. First John 1:7 says, "But if we walk in the light as he himself is in the light, we have fellowship with one another and the blood of Jesus his Son cleanses us from all sin." However, apparently, God allows these angels to at times participate in the process of cleansing his people.

The seraphim remind us to always be zealous in worshiping and serving God. As they cry out to one another in praise, Scripture says we should do the same. In Ephesians 5:18-19, Paul said: "… be filled by the Spirit, speaking to one another in psalms, hymns, and spiritual songs, singing and making music in your hearts to the Lord." As these burning ones lack no zeal in praising and serving God, neither should we. Romans 12:11 says, "Do not lag in zeal, be enthusiastic in spirit, serve the Lord." In addition, the seraphim remind us to be zealous in getting rid of sin in our lives, so God can use us, even as he did with Isaiah. Second Corinthians 7:1 says, "Therefore, since we have these promises, dear friends, let us cleanse ourselves from everything that could defile the body and the spirit, and thus accomplish holiness out of reverence for God." First John 1:9 says, "But if we confess our sins, he is faithful and righteous, forgiving us our sins and cleansing us from all unrighteousness."

The Living Creatures

In Revelation 4:6-9, 5:8, and 15:7, four living creatures are mentioned. Unlike the cherubim who have four faces, the living creatures each have one—the face of a lion, an ox, a man, and an eagle. The living creatures also have six wings, while the cherubim have four. Because they surround the throne of God with the twenty-four elders (Rev 4:4 and 6), who apparently represent redeemed people, some have speculated that the living creatures represent creation before God. The four faces of the lion, ox, man, and eagle represent some of the mightiest representatives of God's creation. Though they look more like cherubim, they act more like seraphim as their chief activity seems to be praising and worshiping God. In Revelation 4:8, they cry out day and night: "Holy Holy Holy is the Lord God, the All-Powerful, Who was and who is, and who is still to come!" Also, in Revelation 5:12, they, along with the twenty-four elders and other angels, declare: "Worthy is the lamb who was killed to receive power and wealth and wisdom and might and honor and glory and praise!"

In fact, the living creatures seem to function like *priestly worship leaders*, initiating heavenly worship. Revelation 4:9-10 says,

> And whenever the living creatures give glory, honor, and thanks to the one who sits on the throne, who lives forever and ever, the twenty-four elders throw themselves to the ground before the one who sits on the throne and worship the one who lives forever and ever, and they offer their crowns before his throne ...

In Revelation 5:8, the living creatures even offer God "golden bowls full of incense (which are the prayers of the saints)." They challenge us to live lives of constant worship—offering our bodies as living sacrifices to God (Rom 12:1) and offering everything we do to the Lord as worship—and they also challenge us to inspire others to worship and glorify God. First Corinthians 10:31 says, "So whether you eat or drink, or whatever you do, do everything for the glory of God." Matthew 5:16 says, "In the same way, let your light shine before people, so that they can see your good deeds and give honor to your Father in heaven."

Conclusion

In Scripture, there are three types of angels. Cherubim, who are mentioned the most in Scripture, are commonly seen guarding the presence of God and the things of God. One was placed in the Garden of Eden to guard the tree of life; two were placed in the holy of holies to guard the presence of God. They remind us to be zealous about guarding God's glory and his worship as well. Worship must be in spirit and truth to be accepted by God (John 4:23), and therefore must be guarded against anything in pretense and that doesn't align with Scripture. Seraphim are only seen in Isaiah 6. They worship God's person and cleanse God's people. They are the "burning ones" who remind us to be zealous in our worship and service and also in cleansing ourselves from sin (Rom 12:11, 2 Cor 7:1). Finally, the living creatures are seen several times in Revelation. They, like the seraphim, continually worship God. They are like God's priestly worship leaders who stay around the throne offering God worship and leading others in the same. They remind us that we are a holy, priestly people who should be consumed with honoring and worshiping God in everything we do (1 Pet 2:9), and leading others to do the same.

Reflection

1. What stood out most in the reading and why?
2. How many types of angels are there and what are they?
3. Describe the types of angels and their functions and share any applications that can be drawn from them.
4. What other questions or applications did you take from the reading?

Specific Angels

Who are the specific angels mentioned in Scripture? There are at least five of them.

Michael

Michael is called "one of the leading princes" in Daniel 10:13 and the "archangel" in Jude 1:9, which demonstrates his rule and authority over other angels.[11] His name means "Who is like God?"[12] He apparently has a specific role in defending Israel. In Daniel 10:21, he is called "your prince" in referring to Daniel and thus Israel. And in Daniel 12:1, it is prophesied that he will protect Israel in a time of persecution during the end-times, which is instigated by the Antichrist. Daniel 12:1 says,

> At that time Michael, the great prince who watches over your people, will arise. There will be a time of distress unlike any other from the nation's beginning up to that time. But at that time your own people, all those whose names are found written in the book, will escape.

Revelation 12:13-14 may also refer to Michael's protection over Israel during the end-times. When Israel, who is referred to as the woman who gave birth to the child (the messiah), is being attacked by the dragon (the devil), she is given wings to fly to a safe place in the wilderness. These wings may refer to Michael helping them (which he may do through some other nation or entity). Revelation 12:13-14 says,

> Now when the dragon realized that he had been thrown down to the earth, he pursued the woman who had given birth to the male child. But the woman was given the two wings of a giant eagle so that she could fly out into the wilderness, to the place God prepared for her, where she is taken care of—away from the presence of the serpent—for a time, times, and half a time.

In the same chapter, Michael is displayed as the leader of the angelic army who fights against Satan and his demons—defeating them and removing them from heaven. Revelation 12:7-8 says,

> Then war broke out in heaven: Michael and his angels fought against the dragon, and the dragon and his angels fought back. But the dragon was not strong enough to prevail, so there was no longer any place left in heaven for him and his angels.

This is not the only time Michael contends with Satan. After Moses' death, Michael argues with Satan about Moses' body. Jude 1:9 says, "But even when Michael the archangel was arguing with the devil and debating with him concerning Moses' body, he did not dare to bring a slanderous judgment, but said, 'May the Lord rebuke you!'" Why was there a dispute over Moses' body? We can only speculate since Scripture is silent on the issue. However, William MacDonald gives a prudent explanation in the Believer's Bible Commentary:

> We have no definite knowledge why the dispute arose between Michael and Satan about the body of Moses. We do know that Moses was buried by God in a valley of Moab.

It is not unlikely that Satan wanted to know the spot so that he could have a shrine built there. Then Israel would turn to the idolatrous worship of Moses' bones. As the angelic representative of the people of Israel (Dan. 10:21), Michael would strive to preserve the people from this form of idolatry by keeping the burial site secret.[13]

In addition, it must be noted that the second coming of Christ will come with a shout from the "archangel." First Thessalonians 4:16 says, "For the Lord himself will come down from heaven with a shout of command, with the voice of the archangel, and with the trumpet of God, and the dead in Christ will rise first." Since no one else is called the archangel in Scripture, this may refer to Michael's role in Christ's coming and the resurrection of the saints.

In Scripture, Michael is a warrior who fights for God's people against the devil and his demons. He reminds us that we are likewise in a spiritual battle. Ephesians 6:10-12 says:

> Finally, be strengthened in the Lord and in the strength of his power. Clothe yourselves with the full armor of God so that you may be able to stand against the schemes of the devil. For our struggle is not against flesh and blood, but against the rulers, against the powers, against the world rulers of this darkness, against the spiritual forces of evil in the heavens.

Even Michael, who is much greater than us, did not rely on his own strength when contending with the devil over Moses' body. Instead, he prayed for the Lord to rebuke him (Jude 1:9). Likewise, Paul said that we can't fight this spiritual war in our own power, we must be "strengthened in the Lord," in "his power," and with "the full armor of God." Certainly, we can only depend on these spiritual resources by constant prayer, time in God's Word, worship, being unified with the saints, and practicing righteousness (cf. Eph 6:13-20).

Gabriel

Gabriel is another angel mentioned in Scripture. His name means "mighty one of God"[14] or "God is strong."[15] He is only mentioned in the books of Daniel and Luke. In both, he is sent by God to give and explain messages to God's people. In Daniel 8:16, he explains the vision of the ram and goat battle to Daniel. In Daniel 9:27, he explains a prophetic vision about Israel's future—including the rebuilding of Jerusalem, the coming of the messiah, the destruction of the temple, the Antichrist, and other end-time events. In Luke 1:19, he predicts the birth of John the Baptist to Zacharias, and in Luke 1:26, he predicts the birth of Christ to Mary.

Gabriel reminds us to always be ready to speak for God and explain his messages to people. First Peter 3:15-16 says, "But set Christ apart as Lord in your hearts and always be ready to give an answer to anyone who asks about the hope you possess. Yet do it with courtesy and respect..." We must always be ready to share the gospel with the lost and help explain away their difficulties with it. We must study God's Word, so we can explain the mysteries of Scripture to believers to aid in their sanctification and to help them trust God more. Second Timothy 2:15 says, "Make every effort to present yourself before God as a proven worker who does not need to be ashamed, teaching the message of truth accurately."

The Angel of the Lord

In the Old Testament, there are many appearances of a specific angel named "the angel of the Lord" who is clearly distinct from other angels (Gen 16:7-12, 21:17-18, 22:11-18, Ex 3:2, Jdg 2:1-4, 5:23, 6:11-24, 13:3-22, etc.). What makes this angel unique is that he identifies himself as God, speaks as God, and exercises the responsibilities of God. Consider two specific examples: In Judges 6:11-16 (ESV), it describes Gideon's call by the Angel of the Lord to lead Israel against the Midianites. It says,

> Now the angel of the LORD came and sat under the terebinth at Ophrah, which belonged to Joash the Abiezrite, while his son Gideon was beating out wheat in the winepress to hide it from the Midianites. And the angel of the LORD appeared to him and said to him, "The LORD is with you, O mighty man of valor." And Gideon said to him, "Please, my lord, if the LORD is with us, why then has all this happened to us? And where are all his wonderful deeds that our fathers recounted to us, saying, 'Did not the LORD bring us up from Egypt?' But now the LORD has forsaken us and given us into the hand of Midian." And the LORD turned to him and said, "Go in this might of yours and save Israel from the hand of Midian; do not I send you?" And he said to him, "Please, Lord, how can I save Israel? Behold, my clan is the weakest in Manasseh, and I am the least in my father's house." And the LORD said to him, "But I will be with you, and you shall strike the Midianites as one man."

Gideon did not initially recognize that this man was an angel, but at some point in the conversation, Gideon recognized that he was in fact the Angel of the Lord and began to cry out with fear to God (v. 22-23). However, what's interesting about this discourse is the fact that the narrator begins to address the Angel of the Lord as God. In verse 14, the narrator says, "the LORD turned to him and said" with capital letters, which means it was God's covenant name YAHWEH. The Angel of the Lord was God.

Likewise, in Exodus 3:1-4 (ESV), the Angel of the Lord appeared to Moses in a fiery bush. It says,

Now Moses was keeping the flock of his father-in-law, Jethro, the priest of Midian, and he led his flock to the west side of the wilderness and came to Horeb, the mountain of God. And the angel of the LORD appeared to him in a flame of fire out of the midst of a bush. He looked, and behold, the bush was burning, yet it was not consumed. And Moses said, "I will turn aside to see this great sight, why the bush is not burned." When the LORD saw that he turned aside to see, God called to him out of the bush, "Moses, Moses!" And he said, "Here I am."

In the story, Moses saw the Angel of the Lord in the bush, and after that, the narrator adds in verse 4, "God called to him out of the bush." The Angel of the Lord and God were the same person.

Many would suggest that when God showed up in the form of the Angel of the Lord, who seemed to always appear as a man, those appearances were actually early sightings of the Son of God. Why do they believe that? It is simply biblical reasoning. After Christ came to the earth, we still have appearances of angels but no appearances of the Angel of the Lord. Also, it would seem logical that since Christ has always eternally existed, he was active and would have manifested himself in the world at various times (cf. John 8:58). Many believe Christ commonly did this as the Angel of the Lord.

Lucifer

Lucifer, also called Satan and the devil (Matt 4:1, 16:23), is a prominent angel mentioned in Scripture. He is the chief evil angel whom we will consider in more depth in Satanology. Isaiah 14:12 (KJV) says, "How you are fallen from heaven, O Lucifer, son of the morning! How you are cut down to the ground, You who weakened the nations!" Lucifer means "shining one" or "star of the morning."[16] Before his fall, he was a cherub who guarded the glory of God and possibly led the angels in worship (Ez 28:13-14 NKJV). In his ministry to God, he became prideful and led one-third of the angels in rebellion, who are now called demons (Rev 12:4). Lucifer's fall is a sobering reminder that it is possible to do ministry with wrong motives and ultimately rebel against God, becoming antagonistic to God, his Word, and his people (cf. Heb 10:29-31). Unfortunately, this has happened to many who previously served in ministry. In 1 Timothy 3:6, Paul warned against placing young believers in church leadership for this reason. He said, "He must not be a recent convert or he may become arrogant and fall into the punishment that the devil will exact."

Abaddon / Apollyon

The final angel mentioned in Scripture is another evil one. His name is Abaddon in Hebrew or Apollyon in Greek—both names mean destroyer. In Revelation 9, it says demonic angels who have been bound in the abyss will be let loose for a short season to judge the earth during the end-times. Abaddon is the leader of these demons. Revelation 9:11 says, "They have as king over them the angel of the abyss, whose name in Hebrew is Abaddon, and in Greek, Apollyon." Some think this angel is Satan; however, he apparently is bound to the abyss until the Great Tribulation. Since Satan is called "the ruler of the kingdom of the air" (Eph 2:2; cf. Eph 6:12) and is not bound to the abyss until the millennial kingdom in Revelation 20:1-3 (cf. Job 1:6-12, 2:1-6), many believe Abaddon is a high-ranking demon bound in the abyss who will lead a demonic invasion to judge unbelievers during the Great Tribulation (Rev 9:4-6).

Conclusion

In Scripture, five angels are mentioned by name—Michael the archangel, Gabriel who is God's messenger, the Angel of the Lord which is probably a pre-incarnate appearance of Christ, Lucifer who is the leader of all demons, and Abaddon who is the leader of the demons bound in the abyss.

Reflection

1. What stood out most in the reading and why?
2. How many specific angels are mentioned in Scripture and who are they?
3. Describe the specific angels and their roles and any applications that can be taken from them.
4. What other questions or applications did you take from the reading?

Closing Principles

What are some closing principles that we should take from our study of angels?

1. We should always stand in awe of the amazing grace we have received in salvation.

Though there was an angelic fall first, God did not send his Son to die for the sins of fallen angels. He simply gave them justice and thereby displayed his holiness. But with humans, God chose to display his grace—his unmerited favor on those who did not deserve it. With that said, God has not only displayed his grace in saving humans but also in the fact that the church has become the body of Christ (Eph 1:21-22, 1 Cor 12:13), is in union with him (Eph 1:3), and therefore is a co-heir with him (Rom 8:17). Because of their relation to Christ, believers will one day have a higher status than angels (Eph 1:20-22, 2:6). In fact, in 1 Corinthians 6:3, Paul said that believers will one day judge angels. Again, this should make believers stand in awe of God's great and gracious plan for sinful humans like us who have repented of our sins and followed Christ as our Lord and Savior.

2. We should be aware, encouraged, and thankful for the daily, unseen activities of angels on our behalf.

In Scripture, angels are mentioned as an encouragement for our daily lives. Again, Hebrews 1:14 says, "Are they not all ministering spirits, sent out to serve those who will inherit salvation?" When we experience God's supernatural protection in a specific situation or sustained good mental and physical health, we should realize that God probably used angels in the process. Psalm 91:10-12 says, "No harm will overtake you; no illness will come near your home. For he will order his angels to protect you in all you do. They will lift you up in their hands, so you will not slip and fall on a stone." In addition, when God gives us special revelation into his Word or guidance for an important decision, it's possible God used one of his messengers to reveal it to us, even as he did throughout biblical history.

Furthermore, every time we enter into worship, Scripture says we enter the heavenly Jerusalem where we worship with angels. Hebrews 12:22-24 says,

> But you have come to Mount Zion, the city of the living God, the heavenly Jerusalem, and to myriads of angels, to the assembly and congregation of the firstborn, who are enrolled in heaven, and to God, the judge of all, and to the spirits of the righteous, who have been made perfect, and to Jesus, the mediator of a new covenant, and to the sprinkled blood that speaks of something better than Abel's does.

When others miss worship or are not passionate in worship, we should be encouraged by the fact that in the spiritual realm, unseen angels sing and worship God with all their hearts along with us.

Also, it is possible that God may send angels to visit us to confirm our obedience or disobedience to his commands. With Abraham, angels visited his house, no doubt, to confirm his obedience to God and bless him (Gen 18). After, they visited Sodom to confirm their immorality and save Lot and his family (Gen 19). No doubt, God may at times do the same with us. The author of Hebrews warns believers about this:

Brotherly love must continue. Do not neglect hospitality, because through it some have entertained angels without knowing it. Remember those in prison as though you were in prison with them, and those ill-treated as though you too felt their torment.
Hebrews 13:1-3

Finally, the presence of angels should also be an encouragement to not sin or be unfaithful in our duties to God. It should always be remembered that angels watch not only our obedience to God but also our disobedience to him. With this in mind, Paul challenged Timothy to faithfully practice church discipline in the church, even when it included disciplining erring elders. In 1 Timothy 5:21, he said: "Before God and Christ Jesus and the elect angels, I solemnly charge you to carry out these commands without prejudice or favoritism of any kind." Wayne Grudem's insights on this are helpful:

> Moreover, we should be aware that angels are watching our obedience or disobedience to God through the day. Even if we think our sins are done in secret and bring grief to no one else, we should be sobered by the thought that perhaps even hundreds of angels witness our disobedience and are grieved. On the other hand, when we are discouraged and think that our faithful obedience to God is witnessed by no one and is an encouragement to no one, we can be comforted by the realization that perhaps hundreds of angels witness our lonely struggle, daily "longing to look" at the way Christ's great salvation finds expression in our lives.[17]

3. We should consider angels as part of our spiritual family— as co-servants and worshipers of God.

Though angels are not part of the church—the body of Christ—they are part of the family of God, since they are called "sons of God" throughout the Old Testament (Job 1:6, 2:1). In Ephesians 3:14-15, when Paul says, "For this reason I kneel before the Father, from whom every family in heaven and on the earth is named," he may be talking about God as Father of all created beings—both human and angelic.[18] Angels are part of God's family and, therefore, our family. Throughout eternity we will serve and worship God together.

4. We should seek to model them in faithful obedience and worship to God.

As mentioned throughout the study, Christ taught that we should pray, "may your kingdom come, may your will be done on earth as it is in heaven" (Matt 6:10). When considering how God's will is done in heaven, certainly this applies to the activity of angels. No matter how mundane or great the task, angels obey swiftly, joyfully, and in a worshipful manner. We must model them in how we serve God and pray that others would do the same.

5. We should never worship, pray to, or seek angels.

Because angels are so awesome, powerful, and glorious, there can be a temptation to worship them. In Revelation 19, John was tempted to worship an angel because of how glorious he was. Revelation 19:10 says:

> So I threw myself down at his feet to worship him, but he said, "Do not do this! I am only a fellow servant with you and your brothers who hold to the testimony about Jesus. Worship God, for the testimony about Jesus is the spirit of prophecy."

Likewise, some Christian groups have errantly prayed to or worshiped angels. Apparently, there were false teachers in Colosse teaching others to pray to and worship angels. In Colossians 2:19, Paul said:

Let no one who delights in humility and the worship of angels pass judgment on you. That person goes on at great lengths about what he has supposedly seen, but he is puffed up with empty notions by his fleshly mind.

Christ is the only mediator between God and man (1 Tim 2:5). There is no need to pray to or seek prayers from angels. In fact, because Jews tended to overly exalts angels, the writer of Hebrews focused on how superior God's Son is. In Hebrews 1:5-14, he said:

For to which of the angels did God ever say, "You are my son! Today I have fathered you"? And in another place he says, "I will be his father and he will be my son." But when he again brings his firstborn into the world, he says, "Let all the angels of God worship him!" And he says of the angels, "He makes his angels spirits and his ministers a flame of fire," but of the Son he says, "Your throne, O God, is forever and ever, and a righteous scepter is the scepter of your kingdom. You have loved righteousness and hated lawlessness. So God, your God, has anointed you over your companions with the oil of rejoicing." And, "You founded the earth in the beginning, Lord, and the heavens are the works of your hands. They will perish, but you continue. And they will all grow old like a garment, and like a robe you will fold them up and like a garment they will be changed, but you are the same and your years will never run out." But to which of the angels has he ever said, "Sit at my right hand until I make your enemies a footstool for your feet"? Are they not all ministering spirits, sent out to serve those who will inherit salvation?

Christ is far superior to any angel because, as God, he created angels. Christ made angels to not only worship and serve him but to serve believers—those who will inherit salvation. We should never worship, pray to, or even seek angels. We should worship, pray to, and seek God (Rev 19:10).

6. We should be cautious about receiving false doctrine from angels.

In Galatians 1:8, Paul warns of this when he said, "But even if we (or an angel from heaven) should preach a gospel contrary to the one we preached to you, let him be condemned to hell!" He warns of this because it is a very real possibility—not that a holy angel would ever teach false doctrine, but a demonic angel would. In 2 Corinthians 11:4, Paul said, "And no wonder, for even Satan disguises himself as an angel of light."

This has happened throughout history in various ways. Joseph Smith, the founder of Mormonism, claimed to have received the insights in the book of Mormon from an angel. Many of the teachings in the book of Mormon contradict Scripture and, therefore, could not have come from a holy angel. Likewise, Muhammad, the founding prophet of Islam, claimed to have received the teachings in the Koran from an angel. We can be sure any insight or revelation from God will never contradict Scripture.

Conclusion

Praise God for his creation of angels! The writer of Hebrews says, "Let all the angels of God worship him!" and "He makes his angels spirits and his ministers a flame of fire" (Heb 1:6-7). Thank you, Lord, for our fellow servants who worship and serve you perfectly. Give us the grace to do the same! Amen!

Reflection

1. What stood out most in the reading and why?
2. In what ways should we be aware, encouraged, and thankful for angels and their activities on our behalf?
3. In what ways should we be cautious of angels or our view of them?
4. What other questions or applications did you take from the reading?

Study Group Tips

Leading a small group using the Bible Teacher's Guide can be done in various ways. One format for leading a small group is the "study group" model, where each member prepares and shares in the teaching. This appendix will cover tips for facilitating a weekly study group.

1. Each week the members of the study group will read through a selected chapter of the guide, answer the reflection questions (see Appendix 2), and come prepared to share with the group.

2. Prior to each meeting, a different member can be chosen to lead the group and share Question 1 of the reflection questions, which is to give a short summary of the chapter read. This section of the gathering could last from five to fifteen minutes. This way, each member can develop their gift of teaching. It also will make them study harder during the week. Or, each week the same person could share the summary.

3. After the summary has been given, the leader for that week will facilitate discussions through the rest of the reflection questions and also ask select review questions from the chapter.

4. After discussion, the group will share prayer requests and pray for one another.

The strength of the study group is the fact that the members will be required to prepare their responses before the meeting, which will allow for easier discussion. In addition, each member will be given the opportunity to teach, which will further equip their ministry skills. The study group model has distinct advantages.

Reflection Questions

Writing is one of the best ways to learn. In class, we take notes and write papers, and these methods are used to help us learn and retain the material. The same is true with the Word of God. Obviously, all the authors of Scripture were writers. This helped them better learn the Scriptures and also enabled them to more effectively teach it. As you reflect on God's Word, using the Bible Teacher's Guide, take time to write so you can similarly grow both in your learning and teaching.

1. How would you summarize the main points of the text/chapter? Write a brief summary.

2. What stood out to you most in the reading? Did any of the contents trigger any memories or experiences? If so, please share them.

3. What follow–up questions did you have about the reading? What parts did you not fully agree with?

4. What applications did you take from the reading, and how do you plan to implement them into your life?

5. Write several commitment statements: As a result of my time studying God's Word, I will . . .

6. What are some practical ways to pray as a result of studying the text? Spend some time ministering to the Lord through prayer.

Walking the Romans Road

How can a person be saved? From what is he saved? How can someone have eternal life? Scripture teaches that, after death, each person will spend eternity either in heaven or hell. How can a person go to heaven?

Paul said this to Timothy:

You, however, must continue in the things you have learned and are confident about. You know who taught you and how from infancy you have known the holy writings, which are able to give you wisdom for salvation through faith in Christ Jesus.
2 Timothy 3:14-15

One of the reasons God gave us Scripture is to make us wise for salvation. This means that without it, nobody can know how to be saved.

Well then, how can a people be saved and what are they being saved from? A common method of sharing the good news of salvation is through the Romans Road. One of the great themes, not only of the Bible, but specifically of the book of Romans, is salvation. In Romans, the author, Paul, clearly details the steps we must take in order to be saved.

How can we be saved? What steps must we take?

Step One: We Must Accept that We Are Sinners

Romans 3:23 says, "For all have sinned and fall short of the glory of God." What does it mean to sin? The word sin means "to miss the mark." The mark we missed is reflecting God's image. When God created mankind in the Genesis narrative, he created man in the "image of God" (1:27). The "image of God" means many things, but most importantly it means we were made to be holy just as he is holy. Man was made moral. We were meant to reflect God's holiness in every way: the way we think, the way we talk, and the way we act. And any time we miss the mark in these areas, we commit sin.

Furthermore, we do not only sin when we commit a sinful act, such as lying, stealing, or cheating. We sin anytime we have a wrong heart motive. The greatest commandments in Scripture are to "Love the Lord your God with all your heart and to love your neighbor as yourself" (Matt 22:36-40, paraphrase). Whenever we don't love God supremely and love others as ourselves, we sin and fall short of the glory of God. For this reason, man is always in a state of sinning. Sadly, even if our actions are good, our heart is bad. I have never loved God with my whole heart, mind, and soul, and neither has anybody else. Therefore, we have all sinned and fall short of the glory of God (Rom 3:23). We have all missed the mark of God's holiness and we must accept this.

What's the next step?

Step Two: We Must Understand We Are Under the Judgment of God

Why are we under the judgment of God? It is because of our sins. Scripture teaches that God is not only a loving God, but he is also a just God. And his justice requires judgment for each of our sins. Romans 6:23 says, "For the payoff of sin is death."

A payoff or wage is something we earn. Every time we sin, we earn the wage of death. What is death? Death really means separation. In physical death, the body is separated from the spirit, but in spiritual death, man is separated from God. Man currently lives in a state of spiritual death (cf. Eph 2:1-3). We do not love God, obey him, or know him as we should. Therefore, man is in a state of death.

Moreover, on the day of our physical death, if we have not been saved, we will spend eternity separated from God in a very real hell. In hell, we will pay the wage for each of our sins. Therefore, in hell people will experience various degrees of punishment (cf. Lk 12:47-48). This places man in a very dangerous predicament—unholy and therefore under the judgment of God.

How should we respond to this? This leads us to our third step.

Step Three: We Must Recognize God Has Invited All to Accept His Free Gift of Salvation

Romans 6:23 does not stop at the wages of sin being death. It says, "For the payoff of sin is death, but the gift of God is eternal life in Christ Jesus our Lord." Because God loved everybody on the earth, he offered the free gift of eternal life, which anyone can receive through Jesus Christ.

Because it is a gift, it cannot be earned. We cannot work for it. Ephesians 2:8-9 says, "For by grace you are saved through faith, and this is not from yourselves, It is the gift of God; it is not from works, so that no one can boast."

Going to church, being baptized, giving to the poor, or doing any other righteous work does not save. Salvation is a gift that must be received from God. It is a gift that has been prepared by his effort alone.

How do we receive this free gift?

Step Four: We Must Believe Jesus Christ Died for Our Sins and Rose from the Dead

If we are going to receive this free gift, we must believe in God's Son, Jesus Christ. Because God loved us, cared for us, and didn't want us to be separated from him eternally, he sent his Son to die for our sins. Romans 5:8 says, "But God demonstrates his own love for us, in that while we were still sinners, Christ died for us." Similarly, John 3:16 says, "For this is the way God loved the world: He gave his one and only Son, so that everyone who believes in him will not perish but have eternal life." God so loved us that he gave his only Son for our sins.

Jesus Christ was a real, historical person who lived 2,000 years ago. He was born of a virgin. He lived a perfect life. He was put to death by the Romans and the Jews. And after he was buried, he rose again on the third day. In his death, he took our sins and God's wrath for those sins and gave us his perfect righteousness so we could be accepted by God. Second Corinthians 5:21 says, "God made the one who did not know sin to be sin for us, so that in him we would become the righteousness of God." God did all this so we could be saved from his wrath.

Christ's death satisfied the just anger of God over our sins. When God looked at Jesus on the cross, he saw us and our sins and therefore judged Jesus. And now, when God sees those of us who are saved, he sees his righteous Son and accepts us. In salvation, we have become the righteousness of God.

If we are going to be saved, if we are going to receive this free gift of salvation, we must believe in Christ's death, burial, and resurrection for our sins (cf. 1 Cor 15:3-5, Rom 10:9-10). Do you believe?

Step Five: We Must Confess Christ as Lord of Our Lives

Romans 10:9-10 says,

> Because if you confess with your mouth that Jesus is Lord and believe in your heart that God raised him from the

dead, you will be saved. For with the heart one believes and thus has righteousness and with the mouth one confesses and thus has salvation.

Not only must we believe, but we must confess Christ as Lord of our lives. It is one thing to believe in Christ but another to follow Christ. Simple belief does not save. Christ must be our Lord. James said this: "…Even the demons believe that – and tremble with fear" (James 2:19), but the demons are not saved—Christ is not their Lord.

Another aspect of making Christ Lord is repentance. Repentance really means a change of mind that leads to a change of direction. Before we met Christ, we were living our own life and following our own sinful desires. But when we get saved, our mind and direction change. We start to follow Christ as Lord.

How do we make this commitment to the lordship of Christ so we can be saved? Paul said we must confess with our mouth "Jesus is Lord" as we believe in him. Romans 10:13 says, "For everyone who calls on the name of the Lord will be saved."

If you admit that you are a sinner and understand you are under God's wrath because of it; if you believe Jesus Christ is the Son of God, that he died on the cross for your sins, and rose from the dead for your salvation; if you are ready to turn from your sin and cling to Christ as Lord, you can be saved.

If this is your heart, then you can pray this prayer and commit to following Christ as your Lord.

Dear heavenly Father, I confess I am a sinner and have fallen short of your glory, what you made me for. I believe Jesus Christ died on the cross to pay the penalty for my sins and rose from the dead so I can have eternal life. I am turning away from my sin and accepting you as my Lord and Savior. Come into my life and change me. Thank you for your gift of salvation.

Scripture teaches that if you truly accept Christ as your Lord, then you are a new creation. Second Corinthians 5:17 says, "So then, if anyone is in Christ, he is a new creation; what is old has passed away – look, what is new has come!" God has forgiven your sins (1 John 1:9), he has given you his Holy Spirit (Rom 8:15), and he is going to disciple you and make you into the image of his Son (cf. Rom 8:29). He will never leave you nor forsake you (Heb 13:5), and he will complete the work he has begun in your life (Phil 1:6). In heaven, angels and saints are rejoicing because of your commitment to Christ (Lk 15:7).

Praise God for his great salvation! May God keep you in his hand, empower you through the Holy Spirit, train you through mature believers, and use you to build his kingdom! "He who calls you is trustworthy, and he will in fact do this" (1 Thess 5:24). God bless you!

Coming Soon

Praise the Lord for your interest in studying and teaching God's Word. If God has blessed you through the BTG series, please partner with us in petitioning God to greatly use this series to encourage and build his Church. Also, please consider leaving an Amazon review and signing up for free book promotions. By doing this, you help spread the "Word." Thanks for your partnership in the gospel from the first day until now (Phil 1:4-5).

Available:
First Peter
Theology Proper
Building Foundations for a Godly Marriage
Colossians
God's Battle Plan for Purity
Nehemiah
Philippians
The Perfections of God
The Armor of God
Ephesians
Abraham
Finding a Godly Mate
1 Timothy
The Beatitudes
Equipping Small Group Leaders
2 Timothy
Jacob
Whenever You Pray

About the Author

Greg Brown earned his MA in religion and MA in teaching from Trinity International University, a MRE from Liberty University, and a PhD in theology from Louisiana Baptist University. He has served over sixteen years in pastoral ministry and currently serves as a chaplain and professor at Handong Global University, teaching pastor at Handong International Congregation, and as a Navy Reserve chaplain.

Greg married his lovely wife, Tara Jayne, in 2006, and they have one daughter, Saiyah Grace. He enjoys going on dates with his wife, playing with his daughter, reading, writing, studying in coffee shops, working out, and following the NBA and UFC. His pursuit in life, simply stated, is "to know God and to be found faithful by Him."

To connect with Greg, please follow at http://www.pgregbrown.com.

Notes

[1] Aaron, Daryl. Understanding Theology in 15 Minutes a Day: How can I know God? Baker Publishing Group. Kindle Edition.

[2] Enns, Paul. The Moody Handbook of Theology (p. 301). Moody Publishers. Kindle Edition.

[3] Aaron, Daryl. Understanding Theology in 15 Minutes a Day: How can I know God?Baker Publishing Group. Kindle Edition.

[4] Enns, Paul. The Moody Handbook of Theology (p. 301). Moody Publishers. Kindle Edition.

[5] Ryrie, C. C. (1999). Basic Theology: A Popular Systematic Guide to Understanding Biblical Truth (p. 153). Chicago, IL: Moody Press.

[6] Grudem, W. A. (2004). Systematic theology: an introduction to biblical doctrine (pp. 401–402). Leicester, England; Grand Rapids, MI: Inter-Varsity Press; Zondervan Pub. House.

[7] Guzik, D. (2013). Mark (Mk 5:9–13). Santa Barbara, CA: David Guzik.

[8] Ryrie, C. C. (1999). Basic Theology: A Popular Systematic Guide to Understanding Biblical Truth (p. 146). Chicago, IL: Moody Press.

[9] Wilmington's Guide to the Bible

[10] MacArthur, J., & Mayhue, R. (Eds.). (2017). Biblical Doctrine: A Systematic Summary of Bible Truth (pp. 669–670). Wheaton, IL: Crossway.

[11] Grudem, W. A. (2004). Systematic theology: an introduction to biblical doctrine (p. 398). Leicester, England; Grand Rapids, MI: Inter-Varsity Press; Zondervan Pub. House.

[12] MacArthur, J., & Mayhue, R. (Eds.). (2017). Biblical Doctrine: A Systematic Summary of Bible Truth (p. 669). Wheaton, IL: Crossway.

[13] MacDonald, W. (1995). Believer's Bible Commentary: Old and New Testaments. (A. Farstad, Ed.) (p. 2342). Nashville: Thomas Nelson.

[14] MacArthur, J., & Mayhue, R. (Eds.). (2017). Biblical Doctrine: A Systematic Summary of Bible Truth (p. 669). Wheaton, IL: Crossway.

[15] Enns, Paul. The Moody Handbook of Theology (p. 303). Moody Publishers. Kindle Edition.

[16] Enns, Paul. The Moody Handbook of Theology (p. 303). Moody Publishers. Kindle Edition.

[17] Grudem, W. A. (2004). Systematic theology: an introduction to biblical doctrine (pp. 405–406). Leicester, England; Grand Rapids, MI: Inter-Varsity Press; Zondervan Pub. House.

[18] MacDonald, W. (1995). Believer's Bible Commentary: Old and New Testaments. (A. Farstad, Ed.) (p. 1929). Nashville: Thomas Nelson.